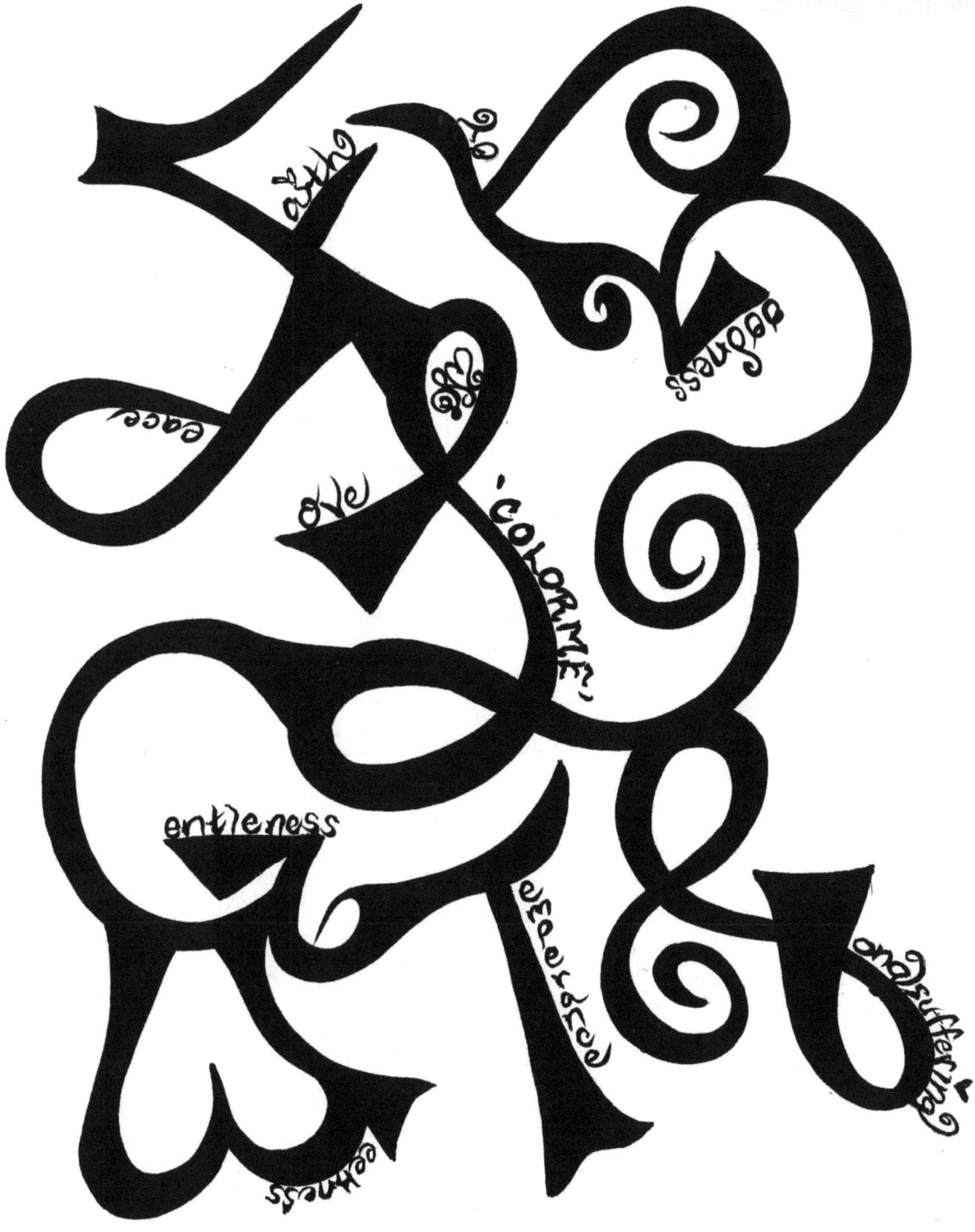

aith
oodness
eace
ove
'COLORME'
entleness
emperance
ongsuffering
eekness

a gift for:

_____

from:

_____

Dedicated to God

Empowering YOU To Creatively

Meditate on God's Word

&

To Find the Artist Within!

Copyright © 2016 Debra Lee Murrow

Published by: COLORME Art Spa, Scottsdale AZ 85255

Design: Debra Lee Murrow

All rights reserved, no portion of this publication may be reproduced, stored in a retrieval system or transmitted in any form by any means - electronic, mechanical, photocopying, recording, or any other - except for brief quotations in printed review, without the prior written permission of the publisher.

Scripture quotations in this book are from the King James Version.

www.DebraLeeMurrow.com

ISBN13: 9780692708149

Printed and bound in the United States of America

Fruits of the Spirit
'COLORME'

More then just a coloring book:)

Coloring Book & Bible Study

By: Debra Lee Murrow

Artistic Bible Lessons Series I

A unique way to experience the Word of God.

This study will change the way you look at worship & the Word.

Instructions

Fruit grown and picked is sweet to the taste and appealing to the eye.
Yet, as Christians we are constantly being challenged by the fruit shared
in the Holy Scriptures.

Galatians 5:22-26 King James Version (KJV)

But the fruit of the Spirit is love, joy, peace, longsuffering, gentleness, goodness, faith,

Meekness, temperance: against such there is no law.

And they that are Christ's have crucified the flesh with the affections and lusts.

If we live in the Spirit, let us also walk in the Spirit.

Let us not be desirous of vain glory, provoking one another, envying one another.

Enjoy creating / coloring on

the Fruits of the Spirit coloring pages.

Feel free to create "outside" the lines, there are no rules:)

Create design with color over the drawings

Express yourself!

These designs are created to ignite decisions of

where and when to start and stop each color

go with the flow let go and let God...

There is no right or wrong only what's right to you

answer the questions on each page of the bible study which is opposite of each

Fruit of the Spirit 'COLORME' Drawing.

To see sample colorings of this book goto:

www.DebraLeeMurrow.com

click Coloring Book

Table of Fruits

Love

Joy

Peace

Longsuffering

Gentleness

Goodness

Faith

Meekness

Temperance

Compilation all 9 fruits

Blank page - Create your own

Love

Write the Fruits of the Spirit scripture: Galatians 5:22 – 26.

Define love

Find and write the scriptures in the drawing
1.

2.

Give an example from your own life of how you have…
1. Shown love

2. Received love

3. Learned love

Do you have love, the first Fruit of the Spirit?

If not, how can I be Love so people can truly see Jesus in me?

_____

Let's pray – Dear Father, in the name of Jesus, I thank you for Love and I desire to be like your son Jesus Christ. I commit to love you Lord with all my heart, mind, soul and strength. I pray that you help me to love my neighbors as myself so everyone can truly see God in me as I walk through my day. Amen.

Joy

Define joy

Find and write the scriptures in the drawing
1.

2.

3.

4.

Give an example from your own life of how you have…
1. Shown joy

2. Received joy

3. Learned joy

Do you have joy, the second Fruit of the Spirit?

If not, how can I have more joy so people can truly see Jesus in me?

_____

Let's pray – Dear Father in the name of Jesus, I thank you for the joy inside me. I desire to be like your son Jesus Christ, for the Joy of the Lord is my strength. I put my trust in you Lord and will show joy all the days of my life. Amen.

Peace

Define peace

Find and write the scripture in the drawing
1.

Give an example from your own life of how you have…
1. Shown peace

2. Received peace

3. Learned peace

Do you have peace, the third Fruit of the Spirit?

If not, how can I have more peace so people can truly see Jesus in me?

Let's pray – Dear Father in the name of Jesus, I thank you for peace within me. I desire to be like your son Jesus Christ, for the peace of the Lord is in me. You Lord give me peace, unlike how the world gives it. I do not let my heart be troubled, and I cast all my cares upon You, because You care for me. Amen.

Longsuffering

Define longsuffering

Find and write the scriptures in the drawing
1.

2.

3.

4.

*Two bonus scriptures

Give an example from your own life of how you have...
1. Shown longsuffering

2. Received longsuffering

3. Learned longsuffering

Do you have longsuffering, the fourth Fruit of the Spirit?

If not, how can I be an example of longsuffering so people truly see Jesus in me?

_____

Let's pray – Dear Father in the name of Jesus, I thank you for longsuffering. I desire to be like your son Jesus Christ, for You gave your only son so none should perish. Jesus was the ultimate example of longsuffering for me and I will always be thankful for where I am and what I have, knowing that You have a plan for me. In due time, I shall be edified in the name of the Kingdom. Amen.

Gentleness

Define gentleness

Find and write the scriptures in the drawing
1.

2.

3.

Give an example from your own life of how you have...
1. Shown gentleness

2. Received gentleness

3. Learned gentleness

Do you have gentleness, the fifth Fruit of the Spirit?

If not, how can I have more gentleness so people can truly see Jesus in me?

Let's pray – Dear Father in the name of Jesus I thank you for gentleness. I desire to be like your son Jesus Christ. Your gentleness in me will make me great and I desire to edify you in my life. I pray that I am gentle with the boldness of a lion and that all men will come to know you Lord. Amen.

Goodness

Define goodness

Find and write the scriptures in the drawing
1.

2.

3.

4.

Give an example from your own life of how you have…
1. Shown goodness

2. Received goodness

3. Learned goodness

Do you have goodness, the sixth Fruit of the Spirit?

If not, how can I have more goodness so people can truly see Jesus in me?

Let's pray – Dear Father in the name of Jesus, I thank you for goodness. I desire to be like your son Jesus Christ. I know Lord that your goodness never leads us astray. I pray that you will show me what I need to repent in my life so that I may dwell in the house of the Lord forever. I revere you Lord, and will keep thy commandments all the days of my life. Amen.

Faith

Define faith

Find and write the scriptures in the drawing
1.

2.

3.

4.

5.

 Give an example from your own life of how you have…
1. Shown faith

2. Received faith

3. Learned faith

Do you have faith, the seventh Fruit of the Spirit?

If not, how can I have more faith so people can truly see Jesus in me?

Let's pray – Dear Father in the name of Jesus, I thank you for the faith within me. I desire to be like your son Jesus Christ. I commit to diligently seek you Lord with all my heart, for I know faith is a gift. I commit to use my faith, which works by love, and help all people understand and use their faith. Amen.

Meekness

Define meekness

Find and write the scriptures in the drawing
1.

2.

3.

4.

Give an example from your own life of how you have...
1. Shown meekness

2. Received meekness

3. Learned meekness

Do you have meekness, the eighth Fruit of the Spirit?

If not, how can I become meeker in my life so people can truly see Jesus in me?

_____

Let's pray – Dear Father in the name of Jesus, I thank you for meekness. I desire to be like your son Jesus Christ. I desire to become your disciple and tell all people about the love of God, as I show meekness unto all men. Amen.

Temperance

Define temperance

Find and write the scriptures in the drawing
1.

2.

Give an example from your own life of how you have…
1. Shown temperance

2. Received temperance

3. Learned temperance

Do you have temperance, the ninth Fruit of the Spirit?

If not, how can I have show more temperance so people can truly see Jesus in me?

Let's pray – Dear Father, in the name of Jesus, I thank you for temperance. I desire to be like your son Jesus Christ. Lord, help me to be last, because the first shall be last and the last shall be first. Show me the patience I need now to lead me to the other fruits. Lord, I pray that I bear much fruit in my life and that it is all of You, because a man that builds a house without the Lord builds it in vain, so I want You to build a house with me. Amen.

'COLORME' Compilation

Love

Joy

Peace

Longsuffering

Gentleness

Goodness

Faith

Meekness

Temperance

**Now it's your turn
create your very own!**

'COLORME' Art Master Piece
on the opposite blank page.

There is no right or wrong,
express yourself.

I believe everyon has a particular style of
fun letter they love to create.
Be bold, be brave, have fun:-)

Remeber to always say,
"I am an Artist & I am Creative"

To Your Success in anything your heart desires!

ABOUT THE AUTHOR

 Debra Lee Murrow is a fine artist, business entrepreneur and the owner and operator of The 'COLORME' Art Spa. She specializes in black & white canvases plus pen & ink, for others to create over her designs and "be the artist". She began her artistic style in 2000 after a revelation of the power of words. This is why her art is comprised of words and phrases mixed together, to create the context of a larger art piece.

Debra's drawings and other artwork is more frequently being classified as "adult coloring". Her 'COLORME' postcards, posters, canvases & necklaces give an interesting twist to any party; birthdays, anniversaries, painting & wine, just for FUN, women's ministries, weddings, rehearsal parties, bar & bat mitzvahs. She also uses her art to help fundraising efforts for organizations. Her work has been displayed and sold at art fairs, silent auctions and artist workshops.

Debra also works with shrink plastic, it's a material you create on and then bake, it shrinks ⅓ and becomes 9x's thinker. Her new line of Healing Heart Necklaces are a favorite. Using this style, Debra creates necklaces, ornaments, birth announcements, room decor and many other fun projects.

As a teacher, Debra has four main workshops: Pen & Ink, Liquid Pouring, Shrink Plastic and 'COLORME' Canvas. She travels to different areas in the world speaking, teaching and inspiring people find the artist within.

To book Debra and learn more about her art work, coaching, speaking, party packages and workshops, please visit her on the web at www.DebraLeeMurrow.com